DOG'S EYE VIEW

ROGER ELKIN

Belfast
LAPWING

First Published by Lapwing Publications
c/o 1, Ballysillan Drive
Belfast BT14 8HQ
lapwing.poetry@ntlworld.com
http://www.freewebs.com/lapwingpoetry/

Copyright © Roger Elkin 2009

All rights reserved
The author has asserted her/his right under Section 77
of the Copyright, Design and Patents Act 1988
to be identified as the author of this work.
British Library Cataloguing in Publication Data.
A catalogue record for this book is available from
the British Library.

Since before 1632
The Greig sept of the MacGregor Clan
Has been printing and binding books

All Lapwing Publications are
Hand-printed and Hand-bound in Belfast
Set in Aldine 721 BT at the Winepress

ISBN 978-1-907276-24-8

CONTENTS

FERNS	7
AFTER THE FIRST BITE	8
MAYFLIES	10
THE ARRIVAL AND AFTER	11
FIRST ROW	12
GILDING THE LILY	14
LOVESONG VARIATIONS	16
THE QUEEN BEE SPEAKS	17
PRO SMOKING	18
ACETYLENE WELDER	20
BIRMINGHAM SHEET PLATER	21
ENGINEERING APPRENTICES	22
BUILDING BLOCKS	23
I PLASTERER	25
II BRICKIE	26
III LABOURER	27
IV PAVER	28
V ROOFER	29
VI ROOFER'S MATE	30
VII PLUMBER	32
VIII PLANNER	33
IX SITE MANAGER	34
PURE AND APPLIED	35
TWO PLUNGES INTO THE SAME POEM:	36
GAME GAME	38
DAN BYRNE'S FAMINE	39
I THE GIFT	41
II DRAWING BLOOD	42
III TAKING SHEEP	44
IV BLACKTHORNS	46
V HUNTER-GATHERER DAN	47
VI DAN'S DIG	48
VII WAITING GAME	50
VIII STINGING PRODDYS	52
IX PALLBEARERS	53
X DAN VIEWS THE ATLANTIC	54

HUNTING WILD	55
OF PERFECTION	56
LOOSFERS CHIL	57
ARNOLFINI VARIATIONS	60
I A WEDDING PORTRAIT	60
II A DOG'S EYE VIEW	62
COMING CLEAR	63
MASQUES	64
CLASSIFIER	65
STORY TELLING	66
ETYMOLOGIES	67
SPOOKY PODMORE	68
THE TROUBLE WITH BEING A W	69
CHRYSANTHEMUM JIM	70
THAT COMMITTEE MEMBER	71
BIG SISTER'S FORMER BOYFRIENDS	72
SALES REP	74
SEPTEMBER SUNDAY	76
ORDERS OF THE GARTER	77
ONCE SNOOKERED, TWICE…	78
VALENTINO'S AQUACLASSES FOR WOMEN OF MIXED NATIONALITY	80
LANGUAGE CLASSES	81
CRITICAL RESPONSES TO ROGER ELKIN'S POEMS	82

ACKNOWLEDGEMENTS

are due to the editors of the following magazines and anthologies where versions of these poems first appeared:

Antigonish Review; Envoi; Equinox; First Time; *Gizza Poem*; Headlock; Orbis; Poetry Ealing; Poetry On The Lake: *Hortus Conclusus*; Psychpoetica; Quantum Leap; Reach; *Routemasters and Mushrooms*; Salopeot; Sarasvati; The Cannon's Mouth; The Journal; *The Machineries of Love*; Ver Poets Competition Anthology 2008; Vigil; Vision On.

IMAGES:
Richard Ansdell: *The Hunted Slaves* XIX Century Source
http://www.art-prints-on-demand.com/kunst/richard_ansdell/hunted_slaves.jpg
Licensing: This image is in the public domain because its copyright has expired.

Jan van Eyck (1387)–(1441) untitled known in English as *The Arnolfini Wedding*, Source The Yorck Project: 10.000 Meisterwerke der Malerei. 2002. ISBN 3936122202.

Other Publications by Roger Elkin include

Poetry

Pricking Out	*(Aquila, 1988)*
Points of Reference	*(Headland, 1996)*
Home Ground	*(Headland, 2002)*
Rites of Passing	*(Shoestring, 2006)*
Blood Brothers, New & Selected Poems (1982-2006)	*(Headland, 2006)*
No Laughing Matter	*(Cinnamon Press, 2007)*

Prose

Critical articles on Ted Hughes in:-

Keith Sagar,	*The Challenge of Ted Hughes,*	*(St Martin's Press, 1995)*
Joanny Moulin,	*Lire Ted Hughes,*	*(Edition du Temps, 1999)*

Eileen's

as ever

"Brothers and Sisters I bid you beware
Of giving your heart to a dog to tear."

Rudyard Kipling

The Power of the Dog

FERNS

Lady-fern and male-fern together
have advanced little further than the cave.
Near cellar-dwellers they eschew sophistication,
prefer conditions to be tough like them.

Civilization's beyond them.
Bare and forked, lean and meanly-housed,
they're down to basics.

There's no pretence;
nakedness is their aim, is their grace.
Reproduction is their lot;
almost animal their lust.

They bed in little comfort,
like it in the nearly dark,
want it long-drawn-out and wet.

Their fingers, limber and fragile,
handle the musk, searching for light,
satisfying their appetite.

Turn them back:
the scores of spores
broadcast their success.

AFTER THE FIRST BITE

After the temptation
after Adam had done as Eve insisted
and the kiss she had burnt deep into his neck
had grown into apple – Adam's apple

After all this and the knowledge of sex
the discovery of the tree in her hand
the wet flower in his
and the awareness of rooting
they attempted to hide

(It was a good job the fig leaf was handy
otherwise bachelor God would have been too embarrassed)

After God had grown anger
and turned them out of the gates
Adam went walking to hide his shame
and Eve sat weeping and weeping outside Paradise

She wept not for ambition – she was proud to have defied
she wept not for knowledge – was pleased to have found out
she wept because outside the gates not one flower had grown
for since the Fall there had only been the fall of snow
its depths a calendar of their fall from grace
and Eve had loved the flowers
that garden   oh that garden

It was too much for God
He sent a messenger in search of her to comfort her

Roger Elkin

Attempting to get things into perspective
God's messenger, being Yiddish, fell back on his resources
used words   they cost nothing
used eyes   they'd been there all the time
used hands   they'd grown with him
(my God, how he used those hands)

It was then a snowflake fell
nestled on his upturned palm
and not wishing his hand to be wet
he breathed on it   blew the snowflake to the ground

and there it rooted

Eve lifted eyes and smiled
"snowdrop" "snowdrop"

She knew she'd win through   she'd survive

and God turned away to save his face

MAYFLIES

are life-prisoners, asylum dwellers released on a day's
parole from their solitary hells, from their padded cells

They're so glad to be together in the outside world
that all of a shimmering quiver they launch a mad rampage

They thaw into flight their frosted wings,
unhinge their cramped restricted limbs,
clear out their fuddled drugged minds
and begin to give their life a meaning

Freedom has gone to their heads
has gone to their brains, their frames
gone to their eyes, their sides, their thighs
to their necks, their chests, their backs, their legs

There's only one outcome for their newfound freedom: Sex
and all their needs   Sex

and all their existence   Sex
before re-entrance
before death-sentence
is all they have   Sex

They know their grace is ephemeral,
coupling is divine, and heaven is   Sex
worth giving up innocence for,
worth doing with fervour

So live and fly   Sex
and fly and die   Sex

Like Eve they fall, they fall, they fall
but have no chance to earn a repeal

They only possess   Sex
between birth and death
what we nearly free men
what we nearly sane men
gained from Eve's freedom   Sex

Sex   Sex   Sex   Sex   Sex   Sex   Sex   Sex   Sex

It'll be the death of them

Roger Elkin

THE ARRIVAL AND AFTER

Now flags are flying,
every bird-call is a trumpet
and the tiny, conquering woman
comes in glory:
even the angels on the roof-tops
are laughing.

But he is boorish,
knocks away her hand
and she abases herself,
salaams to him,
crawls
and then relaxes on the floor.

And all the time his soul
is visible above him
appealing to the gods,
while her face travels
like a spear of passion.

It is a war of nerves;
but it is played
like a sonata for unaccompanied cello,
rippling from the callow opening
through to the jangled ending,
ending in veronal and collapse.

And then two unfulfilled souls
find a mysterious consummation
completing the one
experienced and disturbed
in a sea-swept pool
swaying with weeds
among the fleshy, pink anemones.

Dog's Eye View

FIRST ROW

As she rounds on him, words sail about his ears,
spear above his head, ricochet from walls.
He's not known this side of her before so shares amazement
with the windows, or tries to place himself mentally in corners.

After the first shock, he settles on her looks,
listens with his eyes. He traces the grey that snakes between
her hair; locates the blemish that she missed as make-up glass
made moonscapes of her cheek, blind mountain-lump she pushed
a-rumpling-up; picks out her stabs of tongue, face jugging in
and out; recoils at antagonisms of lip, the upturned
curl, the truculence he always thought had lurked beneath
her courting-kiss; then dares a sideways squinny at her
eyes' manic-flashing at his gaze, a preying-mantis snatch at
his cornea. Those eyes where warmths of love now fury in abuse
slide down cruelling lines at side of nose. Where make-up's run
the joints have slipped, and age is sneaking through.
Satisfied, he fastens on her patchy neck. Inside he sneers.

Meanwhile, she hurls at him his callousness, the piles
of books he leaves around, the mound of rust he calls a car
but doesn't care to clean, the time he wastes just looking into
space, like what he's doing now. He smiles inside.

But hamstrung athlete of her logic's obstacle course, his mind
is torture-track where her charges stretch. Sounds nag at his unease,
ambush his nerve. He cannot hold the fury seizing him: words
spawn inside his bowel, swim up his gut, flounder round the mouth,
leap up and out, a heaving shoal drowning her down with
his syntax's angry river. He angles with her. Barbs and baits,
playing her out till he catches at her glance, and knows
she, too, is listening with her eyes.

Roger Elkin

Words flip-flap before their sense; flail to a stop.

He numbs to quietness. She checks. It dawns -
anguishes of time. Inadequacies of words. The brevity
that life has granted them to know each other has shown
they barely knew themselves, but clutched at what they hoped
was there, a sympathy.

She smiles, and, as she smiles, she's prettying now. He laughs.

Hands stretch out to heal the wound that words have bruised on air,
to resurrect their pride, to build their masks again.

Dog's Eye View

GILDING THE LILY

I   *Budhead*

      That swelled pod greenhorning to fulness till
      verging on bursting under potentials of yet to come
      like that pubescent lad seen nude on the shoreline
      his prick rising to manhood though no pubic haze,
      just skin with its opaline sheen like china
      and its pinking angry glans...

      Stroke it. As a youth, you, too, knew
      such smooth-hardness, that arcing curve, that ache
      pushing to a bruising juice, that lift of arrival.

II   *Bulbs*

      Close eyes. Feel deep in that darkness.
      Root in the bag. Imagine you're sliding
      the fly, hands in pants in the dark, or in bed
      when you can't rock off to sleep so toss and turn
      trying to occupy mind finding the words to write this.

      C'mon man: you've cupped bulbs like this – almost –
      as fingers resting the weight, thumb stroking scrotum
      you've plumbed for lumps in face of the big C fear.

      So, scan with your touch:
      make sure they're firm, unblemished, whole,
      then share the awareness that beneath wrinkled skin
      generations muster in stirrings of seed.

III   *Basal Scale*

Roll it – hard – between finger and thumb.
It owns that cold-marbled feel of was-it-Anne's
fifteen-year-old nipples as under a chill October moon
after the Youth Club you unclipped her bra-clasp to tremble
firm breasts. For her, thin girl of the Council Estate
with the face of ten-a-day-fags, coke and chips,
it was a been-there affair. For you, your first time:
the route to dreams of any and every wench's cunt.

Let's have it off, then.   Reproduce.   Multiply.

IV   *Flower*

The decadent scent's reminiscent of the perfume
from the mussed hair of Janice, that one night stand
you managed during the management weekend.

How her smell haunted head for days, short-circuiting
desk-thoughts, mind reeling in trouser-rising wetness;
how it seized attention hearing the kids' reading, the wife longing;
how it prolonged the long nights draining of sleep...

And the satin-cold of its petals:
her wet-mouth-corner kiss, her clitoris-slipperiness;
her breasts' waxed sheen...

The whole gaping face of it, tight-lipped, dumbstruck till now:
her harlot mouth with its tarty lipstick
and that fixed slash of a smile dragging down
through its must of musk to the vulva's pulsing wound
          – *yes*   <u>*yes*</u>   *YES* –
in that bright-eyed heart-racing mind-blowing moment
of going over the top.   Again and again.

And again and again, she kept coming – no kidding –
with the drive of this flower, its exotic aroma,
its lusting for life in orgasm of being.   Its need.

LOVESONG VARIATIONS

I   Watching her dressing this morning
I saw she wore my beard between her thighs.

Panicked into sweat, I fingered chin
and found her electric fuzz
triangling round my lips. Amazed,
I claimed she'd preyed on me
while I lay fast asleep.

She laughed, then said
    — *Didn't I know I'd had her heart for years?*

II   Watching him dressing this morning
I saw he wore my beard between his thighs.

Panicked into sweat, I fingered chin
and found his electric fuzz
triangling round my lips. Amazed,
I claimed he'd preyed on me
while I lay fast asleep.

He laughed, then said
    — *Didn't I know I'd had his heart for years?*

III   Watching me dressing this morning
he saw I wore his beard between my thighs.

Panicked into sweat, he fingered chin,
and found my electric fuzz
triangling round his lips. Amazed,
he claimed I'd preyed on him
while he lay fast asleep.

I laughed, then said
    — *Didn't he know he'd had my heart for years?*

Roger Elkin

THE QUEEN BEE SPEAKS

Am too worn now for swarming,
so have made death untenable
with devotions to giving birth.
My being is egg-machine.

Every minute brings addition:
white sliding capsules
each cocooned to a honeycomb
in the round skep's assembly-gloom.

My handmaidens – uncountable
hundreds – are bent on virginity,
their genitalia traded for tail-end regalia
crowned with stings of hooks.

Spinsters insistent on innocence,
they suckle the nursery larvae
on royal jelly, go questing for nectar
in replication of selves.

Are secretive: hold the whereabouts
of clover, of heather
hidden in the riddles
of their zizzing dance.

Deep indoors, conspiracies
of drones interrogate their sex
in election of fathering
the next queen.

The sole use of males
is divining patrimony.
Feeding their machinations on may-bes,
I keep them on hold.

PRO SMOKING

Between men, she straightens up tights and her face
Where the seams peel away, hitches her tits,
Drags hands through hair, and picks up cigarettes.

                    There's Craven A.

The flip-top pack is seduction-box
Raising the fly lodged in her chest,
Climbing her throat till its flapping-wings
Tickle teeth and tongue to buzz bad-breathed
Out of her lips.

                    Senior Service the tar
                    Of an old profession like her.

She pivots the white pleasure-stick,
Pivots and dandles it. Has handled so many
Her eyes need not look. It's as soulless as work
Always knowing what to expect.

                    Players Please: more kicks
                    From No 10 than No 6.

She rolls the spatted end, the stiff finger.
Fish-nicotine smell, kipper-tanned
On her hands, she toys with its cylinder,
Pushes and pulls – dildo for the other end.
Mouth-vagina kisses and wets;
Clitoris-tongue snails up its tip;
Desire is stretched to her uterus-lungs.

                    Dicapilly and Dark Prive
                    Confusing love.

Eye tracing snakes on faded wallpaper,
She pulls and she drags; inhaling life in a fire,
Pulling it all deep down inside her,
Exhaling death in her breath.

                Has Camel,
                the beast with two backs.

In minutes it's done. Pale scatter of ash;
Flat-crampled butt, wet-end and wasted,
Sagkneed in the ashtray's blind eye;
Lipstick-smudge all she's given away.

                Work is a drag;
                Life is a fag.

Between cigarettes, mouth tasting the iron of boredom,
Empties out ash, splashes fresh perfume,
Remakes her lips, and picks up her men.

                Knows well enough
                Wives can damage her wealth.

ACETYLENE WELDER

Nurtured for years on tales of angels,
of gods, of things bringing outward signs
we have gazed on moons, on stars, on suns
and turned our eyes and minds
from such a sight as this – a man
creating universes of his own.

Alone on these dark parabolas of steel
his torch pours out a galaxy
of interstellar activity,
circumvents a new blackhole,
spawns a clutch of asteroids
and highlights a second stellar pole.

Within afternoons he's outshone
the Great Bear, even old Orion,
and formed fresh constellations
curving through the dark unseen.

Will all his work reach out to touch infinity?

Perhaps his God is even such a one –

each falling down of dusk
a pulling on His mask
to create far stars that shine
beyond limited horizons.

Of such acts as this we formulate theology.

Of such mankind, we make an unsung deity.

BIRMINGHAM SHEET PLATER

His is no stage-setting for a western Noh play,
no eastern-bloc cooperative drama,
no cardboard flat or film set, no painted backcloth
of second generation realism:
those gussets and fillets of steel, those girders and plates,
rib-structures and struts, are for real – his props
in a final act of the last ditch stand of tradition.

If he's actor at all, it's an inherited role
hammed down the generations, cast by Darby of Coalbrookdale,
refined by Huntsman, prompted by keeping Kaiser Bill at bay,
perfected by guesswork and the toll of the Atlantic,
rehearsed in the furnaces of Europe
and written down by the Wall Street crash when his mates
understudied their youth in jobbings-out, till Chamberlain
fell foul to the denouement of peace, and steelyards
rang to the falling clangs of tonnage.

The iron has entered his veins, the darkness his hands.
His submission to steel almost suicidal.
Taking strain, muscles splay the lay of spiced rope.
His only vice is his grip, that lock-snap-hold that keeps him humble
though he will never go down.

Optimistic as steel, stubborn as cleats, though Empires decline
his gauntlet still holds firm against Jap technology,
cheap Korean labour. His skill is his will, made immune
to defeat on the smeltings of time, and the grandeur of cranes.

Though bow shackles accept tear-dropped slings
there'll be no compromise for this Brummie Samurai;
no denying, save at drinking-up time in *The Welders' Arms*
when Keir Hardie's ghost moves his mates
to keep the red flag flying.

ENGINEERING APPRENTICES

They might well be Elizabethan blades, swaggering in blacks
and leather, and thrusting their knotted codpiece of genitals
as proof of pedigree. Aspiring turners, they are the stabbing jacks
of the workshop, perfected on the cut and thrust of steels.

Wearing suspicion in their eyes at the elegance of words,
and unconcerned with the genealogy of the bastard-file,
their morality marked by the micrometer, they round their deeds
on the drama of the lathe, the denouement of swarf.

As cavalier as starlings, a petrol-clad rabble that chatters down
the town, street mobsters who gain identity by sharing it with
others, is it more than youth they lose on the Wall of Death?
More than manhood they find behind the Ghost Train?

Because they carry proof of their deeds in the spoil of their hands
you know there's always engineering apace.
So see them as the Bosola of the boilerhouse,
or some other villainous wag – Iago, Mosca, Subtle, Face.

Each generation needs have its hirelings;
each age, its engineering knave.

Roger Elkin

BUILDING BLOCKS

Dog's Eye View

Roger Elkin

I   *Plasterer*

Colt of a youth, he's finding his legs in this world,
so most of the time stands uneasily on the edge of
things, shifting weight from foot to foot. Listening.
And smiling. Has problems forming thoughts as words,
so parrots, with lots of laughter. Not in his eyes, though:
they're flat and sad, sometimes afraid like a lad out of
his water-depth. That's when he yens for a rollup – so
it's out with the Rizlas and the plastic tobacco packet,
and quick as a finger-flip and wet-lip-swipe he's got
a fag on. His face landslides to ease. Knows we don't
smoke, so is convinced we're missing out; grows smug.

Lean as the wind, works like a trooper. Purpose and need
unleash him to action. From mixing the pink plaster dust
through to feathering, he's possessed. Pushing and holding;
caressing and sliding; stroking, smoothing, and gliding till
finishing off. Look at his eyes; how they light. Miss nothing:
lingering on the fingering of surfaces, like skin. He's good,
and knows it:
          Touch of class, that. Visibly grows. And glows.

Shame, then, he's fallen into the trap of the trade. Already
has its hallmark: **Dad** and **Mam** picked out in black at the back
of each wrist; British bulldog glowering over right shoulder;
the pissed-with-his-mates joke, **Made In England**, at his waist;
on left forearm his name – **Jimmy** – in Chinese; and on the right,
Nicky his girl in fancy script *so if we finish it can be turned to
Celtic scrolls.* For the moment, though, is travelling hopefully.
Gets married next Saturday:
          Stag night tonight. Legless. Again.
Is laughing, now, at his own joke:

          Be well and truly plastered!

Dog's Eye View

II   *Brickie*

One of the old school, arrives early, and sits patiently waiting
in his estate, picking off the minutes with the Sports reports
and the sneakiest of peeks at Page Three. Once on site, is first
to start work. No stop for a brew, and none throughout the day;
never smoked; doesn't break for lunch, but keeps a steady pace
shared out between mixing and laying. You can feel the courses
rising almost out of his hands, as if by levitation. Watching him
is magic. Mortar circling like a cow-splat on his board, he lifts
his trowel; digs, twists, turns and folds; then slices off a stiff-soft
tranche that he moulds almost like an ice-cream wafer, smoothing
off the wedge of edge and butting-up against yesterday's build.
It's the splish of washing-up liquid that does the trick. That, and
practice. Almost fifty years have distilled his skill to something
approaching intuition: can nick and chip the brick exactly to shape
for cutting-in with neat flicks of his sharp trowel; the rack of his eye
underwrites plumb-line and spirit-level; his pointing is perfection.

Can't stand waste, so cadges off-cuts of wood from window-props
and cut-off joists. *Asking's better than taking. Making a shed-floor.*

At sixty-four, couldn't live with retirement. Has bricking in his blood;
his bones. Dreams of being barrowed off site, dumped in a skip and
rumbled away to some in-fill, somewhere. Useful till the last.

III   *Labourer*

Doesn't give a shit for building, though without him –
    trench-digger, cement-mixer, barrow-handler, skip-filler,
    mortar-carrier, water-hoser, brick-picker, tea-maker,
    thumper-down-of walls with his lump-hammer,
    not to mention can-you-juster, gofer, dog's body -
the whole build already filling months not weeks
would last much longer. Truth is, he thinks he's top dog.
Is, almost. With his bevelled cannon-ball head on his thick-set neck,
his grimaced chisel jaw, and frame narrowing to his waist,
he's spitting image of bulldog Spike from ***Tom and Jerry***.

All jigged up, his eyes flick nervously. He never settles;
speaks in rattles – and riddles – sentences ending mid-air.
Has to say most things again. Again. His words hack at you
madly, like plasterer's tacks. Doesn't give a toss for pc speak.
Calls a spade a *bloody spade. Besides there int many effin' Pakis
in buildin'. Got more effin' sense. Know whar I mean.*

No wonder, then, he doesn't give a shit for building
though he'd be the first to admit he's built like a back-yard privy
with boulders for shoulders honed three nights a week
pumping muscle, flexing pecs, and gripping his tin-can six-pack belly
at the **Gym'll-Fix-It Leisure Club** (members only),
then fine-tuned the rest of the week on T-bone steaks,
donner-kebabs and lukewarm Stella.

Lives for football: *That's for real.* Man Utd fan like his son
it's for him, not his lad, that he's rendered the gable-end
and painted a huge team-shield with legend in red and white.
*Better than that Paddy bastard crap. All guns and balaclavas.
I'm for effin' England. Who effin' needs new Labour: bastard crap.*

IV   *Paver*

His soft voice, soft hands and softer eyes, sky-bluely smiling,
make Dave something of a misfit in this building trade
designed to reap fast bucks and bugger customers up.

Decades away, he'd have been farm-labourer
herding cattle and sheep, tending hens and geese
in some hillside village nestled just under the hill-ridge
with the ring of moorlands to all horizons,
the network of drystone walling, and wider skies
lit in brilliant sunlight or drowned in cloud and mist.

You can see his affinity with stone
in the way he handles these setts:
caressing their faceted shapes, scuffing off earth-dirt,
dressing edges with his chipping chisel,
turning them, like precious bowls, in his hands
and placing them delicately, but firmly –
just there – and there – with all the skill of a man of the land,
inherited rather than learned.

Ribbed for being *daft bastard – slow – a lazy git*
his is steady, patient work, taking days till the driveway
is paved: a quiet, dignified job done by a gentle man,
soft of tongue and thankful for lack of rain.

V   Roofer

Parks his trannie – *Just for the hell of it!* – so it juts across
our neighbour's drive, then stands having the last drags
of his fag and smiling at what his young lad has drafted
in dust on the back of the van: *Also in white. Clean me!*

Once up our path and past the bricks, wood and sand he's raring
to go – *Oh for home. Only joking, chum!* – but you wouldn't know
what with the standing and staring; chatting and fagging; flapping
hands; miming a brew; bantering with mates. Anything to stretch
the job out, make us wait. It's the builders' game: question of power:
craft chasing cash, engineered to get us eating out of their hands.

But once Mal starts, he's all speed. And ease: a sort of grace, even.
Take the way he handles ladders: carries them over his shoulder,
then angles them, finely – as if they were glass – against girders
and joists. See how his toes tap the rungs in a Fred Astaire routine –
nimble, rhythmic – so before you know it he's up there, balancing on
rafters and purlins, and piecing together his progress, boots tracing
a soft-shoe shuffle across ridgebeams – no wobbling, no hard-hat
or harness, just a mason's apron, nails between teeth, claw-hammer
to hand, and feet at slightest degrees from vacancies where space
gapes beneath. Doesn't admit to doubt or fear: knows only cool.
Watch him dealing out pan-tiles as if for a game of Patience; then
cutting the selvedge by rule of sight to fit in mastery of angles.

True iceberg of a man, there's more to him than meets the eye,
like that tip-tail tattooed at his navel that has you imagining
its triangular pattern zigzagging down his groin to become
a one-eyed trouser-snake. Reading your mind, his face breaks
into smiles: *You guessed! Raised more than roofs. Ask the wife!*

Dog's Eye View

VI   *Roofer's Mate*

Takes ages in the transit van,
mobile clamped to the side of his head,
mouth opening and closing as if he's got earache,
but he's busy dishing it out, saving face
with his woman: *Course I lurv you, Jill.*
Effing lurv you. Climbs smouldering down,
eyes glazed, hurt-boy look, scowling brows – till suddenly
lifts, shrugs head, grows lupine, rolling under
his shoulders, louring down the drive, ready to start.
Another job. Another day. Dreaming backhanders.

Confronts, face to face: *Brew on, then?*
Glint chip of gold tooth; lips smiling like a chisel,
eyes mean as a mean weasel's. Steel bright.
Thinking himself a looker, becomes a looker.
Cock-sure, would charm the knickers off
your daughter, your wife; shag you if he could,
shag anything on two legs.

Driven by his groin since puberty,
has lived perpetual confession, wrangling with guilt
courtesy of *his enema, the Pope.* So is tattooed
with bent head of Christ and, beneath,
Dürer's *Praying Hands*, but put out of his sight
behind him. Like the writing at the base of his head:
CUT ON DOTTED LINE_ _ _   As if!

Thinks he's living out Soaps. For real. Now, under sun,
he's in *Bay Watch*. Top off, fancying his chances:
the moment's Adonis. Strokes his arm lovingly,
finger tracing out *Billie* in copper-plate.
Has fitted their bedroom with white carpet.
Shag, natchrally. 'Er indoors lurvs it.
Gives himself stiffies just thinking of it.

Roger Elkin

Fag on, demands more tea. Smokes as if his life
depended on it. Flips his smouldering butts
to burn holes in our roses. Never asks for the lav,
but arse-ends it around the garden-wall corner
where the moss yellows in betrayals.
Thinks we haven't noticed.
His eyes give nothing away.

VII *Plumber*

What would he think if he knew
my wife had said he works like a dancer?
What would Rob say?

It's the way he lays out his tools –
spanners, wrenches, drills
and spaces them precisely
as if he's measured the distance
separating them.

Not that only, but how he paces the job:
an ordered routine he's waltzed his way through
in endless rehearsals
until perfected to a state of balance and poise
that verges on agility.

See the way he leans
feeding the piping through his hands,
sashaying the radiator across the room,
and handling spanners to tighten valves.
Even putty in his hands follows where he leads.
And his feet have that dancing lightness of touch,
that rhythm of dance.

Do you think he'd be flattered?
Embarrassed? Consider her potty?
Say *Whata loada ballcocks!* (under his breath)
but smile at her – nicely, nicely –
then continue dancing out the day,
locked in his own pipe-dreams?

VIII   *Planner*

a dapper man: Mr. Neatness
in creased trousers and shiny shoes, soft-toed,
so no-one knows where he's coming from

plots out our needs with his black attaché case,
grin-hinged clipboard and tape-measure that slices
light and air, rapier-like, to centimetres

keeps the world's misrule at bay
by reducing it all to scale:

    A5 for outlines/sketches/estimates
    A4 the floor plan, with windows/doors
    A3 complete with peaked gable-ends
    A2 underscored in longhand marking the facts of things:
    brick and thermal block; hang-tile and pan-tile;
    RSJs/timber beams/steel lintels;
    strengths/lengths/dimensions/bearing loads;
    Visqueen and Velux; insulation and finish

never makes A1: too much a calculating-master for that:
calm, and – yes, you guessed? – measured:
almost two-dimensional;
lacking depth, leaves everything to the imagination

downsizes the present by always looking to the future
and not seeing things how they really are;
does all things according to plan

builds his creed on foundations of concrete screed
and the trinity of British Standards, building regs
and need-for-cash-up-front

ensures his erections get approval:
hangs out, regularly - nudge, nudge, say no more –
with a man from Planning:
knows he'll mostly succeed

IX   *Site Manager*

There's never any way you'd catch him with his shirt off:
he's far too conscious of his rank to reveal a naked chest.
In fact, keeps himself apart not only in his dress but in his
speech: uses terms like *the integrity of the house*, *aesthetics*,
incumbent on the firm in cadences that are more at home with
salesman's pitch than building-sites. It's verging on a sort of
verbal diarrhoea that's designed to ridicule the customer and
intimidate his work-mates. Do they suspect, like us, that these
nice-sounding words are just bull-shit: a crafty stratagem to
save his face? Is that why they smirk so much? We know that
planning schedules, ordering materials, flattering inspectors
outdo the need to work up sweats, and strip – and that by never
exposing self beyond shirt sleeves he both covers his back and
manages a fresher sight: the striking absence of tattoos!

PURE AND APPLIED

That adolescent lad just granted crutches
to help his lagging leg is happy to be centre
of his friends' attention. Swinging geometry
into public gaze, he's theorem without paper,
hung on supports, a fixed foot, cantilevered;
or huger insect thing sporting bravery
divided between his shoulder blades.

As leg mends and he inclines to manhood,
he'll lean casually to marriage
where privately, his arms stretched like insect wings
               his navel the nut keeping him together
               his legs dividing the angle of hers
               his desire held at exact right angle
               his arc segmenting her triangle
square rooted to the spot,
he'll work out answers on his young wife's crutch

and be amazed to find the sum of parts
is sometimes greater than the whole.

Dog's Eye View

TWO PLUNGES INTO THE SAME POEM: STAINFORTH FALLS WITH LADS DIVING

I   California University he sports on his sweatshirt
lying on the limestone pavement with its clints and grykes,
though this is the furthest West he's been –
home and England.

A tautened bow, spine zipping his back from just above
his trunks to his shoulder blades, a haze of hair blurring
his clean-lined frame, he stands at the waterfall edge.

What he has to conquer is not the twelvefoot drop
between edge and pool, but the depth of his imagination,
for, though upstream the river is clear as beer in the shallows,
there, beneath the fall, it is brownyblack as stout
and he's drunk on it.

How deep it reaches is beyond his thinking.
In testing water is finding self by conquering the doubts
nagging in his mind. So it is his imaginings he plumbs,
and the fear is not of diving, but of not being able
to perfect the dive.

His eyes search out the place where water will embrace him.
He concentrates, like setting a girl, lifts arms
as in some ancient sort of praise, tries toes for balance,
leans forward, rocks back, and then resets his feet.

This is his masterpiece: the time before the dive
when every muscle is fired to draw attention to the plunge.

Heels rise slightly, toes take the strain.
A spring runs through his calves, tension rippling his body,
ligaments and muscles stretch.

He lifts, arms quickening together, arcing into light.
He streams through space leaning on air,
but the eye cannot accommodate his dive.
Over and done before…

II Asked to record the colour of this river –
its shallows, beer-clear; falls a bitter-brown;
and its transparency cupped within his hands –
this fourteenyearold would reach for blues
as in his junior school days: no way would
he believe what is really there. His excuse?
His sole concern is perfecting dives. That's
what's dragging him, time after time, till he's
light-headed with water's intoxicating swirls.

His body angling Braquelike, he's sapling;
and its planes, shapes, patches, squares seem
etched out of space, his lean limbs shaded in
with hairlines so fine they're barely there:
no hint of the rotund bole he might become.
Even his sex is shelved. The care he took
in choosing trunks that shove his knot of
genitals up front has been immersed in dive's
refinement. So in firming-up his manhood,
it's in water, not in flesh; for these casual
passers-by, not self, or folk up close to him.

See his stylish dive: shoulders panning out
to manikin, as back held taut, square-cut,
he tarzans from the swinging rope: a collapsing
flash against the light. And before you blink,
this kingfisher-lad has splashed through water's
silk meniscus – and out again – river-pearls
blistering skin, and glistening under leaning sun.

GAME GAME

Rabbids he says, unannounced at our back door,
his Asda carrier-bag sagging under the weight
of their lumpy forms, and dried blood smudging
its creased polythene with swipes of browny-red.

In a mix of nervous pride and tease, he half-thrusts
this sudden gift then withholds as if unsure, till
almost juggles his catch to my outstretched hands.
'Ems gutted, he says. *Dressed?* I tease, expecting him
to be unsure with words. *Yup. Gutted.* His eyes dead.

Not knowing me yet, he's edgy as moorland fields
when the buzzards wheel, so is giving nothing away,
but nudges closer, shuffling his muddy boots and
wheedling a way in as though he finds the vacancies
of personal space threatening. His face is motionless:
has that same scared-rabbit look of things he's shot
as if someone else is working his lips, and making
his eyelids blink. Meantimes, I'm thinking of the job
close to hand: sawing at throats, their heads statuesque
in deadness, eyes stone still; bodies stretched full length
with legs caught mid-leap to safety; snicking off velvet
feet; disrobing pelts like tight gloves; then wiping away
veils of blood from knives, hands and fingernails.

And, suddenly, I surprise us both by looking at him,
tracking up his face, noticing how his eyes switch on
when I slip him a couple of quid. *See you next week?
Same time.* But as I make to put the door on its latch,
he's ahead of the game: his boot already in the gap. *Yup.
Wud-pidgins, or-right?* I nod eagerly. *Gutted, innit?*
Yes. Gutted. He shifts foot, licks lips, and turns. *Or-right.
See yer then, then.* Knows he has me in his sights again.

Roger Elkin

DAN BYRNE'S FAMINE

Dog's Eye View

I   The Gift

This lazy-bed was long past raiding, the spuds gone rotten-soft,
their tell-tale stink keeping folks away for weeks, but that Friday
Michael, Patrick and Dan were magnetised by a riddling haze of flies,
their iridescent scarab-greens and wet-pebble blues, and that bizzing
niggling away at sanity like hunger pangs, till rising in clouds
when the lads arrived, arms thrashing widely and whooping at what
they'd found: a dead fox with curved black paws and ochre claws,
lying curled and bloodied like a stillborn child.

                                        Eyes dead and hard as glass,
his head was jarred against the body's rhythm, torso madly-angled
and framed in pain, with brown blood-streak slipping down his snout
from between the teeth's manic flash of grin, his hip twisted where
he'd struggled to free his right hind-leg from the jagged man-trap
snagging at his shank's bronze-copper, the colour already fading
from his russet pelt, the blood smudging the vest of his chest and
his rust-red shoulder where he'd snapped and bitten in his anguish,
his flank draining to paler brown: all his burnished majesty dished out
between pain and death.

                                   It wasn't till Dan shifted him –
kicking first, then bending, and nudging gently, animal-like, insistent,
at the body's ironsides – that the foot-long spikes designed to deter theft
and spear feet were seen, now piercing the fox's guts where he'd lashed
angrily in his freedom-fight, jagging first this way, then that. Retching
at the writhe of maggots, Patrick and Michael lifted him clear of the stakes,
then tackled the man-trap's spring.

                                   Today, for once, there would be
no fighting. The rituals of townland life insisted that this fox would be
wrestled free; every piece of him collected, kept safe, and shared between
the Reilly lads and Dan; then taken home to folks beside themselves
with relief at this gift of food: the first meat they'd feasted on in weeks.

"*Local tradition... still recalls fights over the bodies of foxes.*"
Roger McHugh, **The Famine in Irish Oral Tradition**, *(1956), page 402*

II *Drawing Blood*

Was late March, around about five, the sun near setting,
when the Reilly brothers, Michael and Patrick, stood tall,
jars to hand, in Dan Byrne's yard, with their frisky stirk
spragged firm between them, spittle dribbling from its lips
and hanging on its amber coat – rough-plush and long –
horns just forming, pushing stumpy through.

The stirk's first time, it sensed the worst; could smell
spilt blood on the packed mud floor, so was restless –
smouldering and wanting to bolt, shouldering forwards
and back in a sort of reel-become-jig – the three lads shifting feet –
its stamping hooves, dust flying, head rising, then down again,
agate eyes rolling – wide, wild – snorting, and riffling,
and splaying its forelegs, lowering the whole of its body –
then tossing head back up again, triumphant, resisting –
breath caught, haloing, in the lamp's flickering.

Patrick stalling the stirk's struggling haunches against the wall,
and Michael cradling its anvil-head, Dad Byrne took a knife, and
dragged it against his thumb's run; turned it, glinting; whetted it;
then cleaned the blade on his sleeve. Dan readied the quart-jug,
and waited – held breathing – for the fall of that heavy quietness
before the slicing cut, nicking the snaking neck vein – blue-black –
the sudden head wrench – eyes writhing – Michael holding fast –
and quick spurts of rich blood, velvet-thick, till hot and gushing,
Dan nudging the jug to catch it – fresh blood-stars littering the yard
and glistening in the guttering light – all the time the stirk shifting
the rhythm of its being the length of its flank as, living its life-dance,
it tried defiantly to lift its head, stretching neck to bellow, Michael
hanging on. Worst was the stopping – always difficult pushing
that first pin across the incision, knitting skin together – more bucking –
the four of them soothing, and stroking, till Patrick passed the strands
cut from its tail and Byrne plaited them, lapping, around the pin –
the lowing moans – its drum pulse – shivers rippling its frame –
all that surging weight being whispered down to stillness.

Wiping hands, Byrne racked the knife, then sloped indoors,
leaving behind the iron smell of blood – steam rising – as Dan poured
into jars for the Reillys to trophy back home, melting silently
through the night to their worry of starving kids, and Mary
to boil with milk, oats, cabbage stalk and herbs, then shape into
"relish cakes" for frying – and the hurt stirk put to the out-field
where the wound would grow whole again, till next time.

"A man... brought... cows to my father's father to draw blood for his starving family, about a quart from each cow."
Irish Folklore Commission, Cork Archive, Responses J

III Taking Sheep

Ribbons of snow limning the hedgerows, Michael and Dan
lay low in the gorse, its unseasonal sulphur buds smudging through
dark green spikes, while Patrick singled out this thistle-blinded ewe –
One eye is addled. Be easy as breathing. The other two agreed –
We'll take her. Easy – lean and battered by wind, half-starved like them,
scraggy beneath raggy coat, with nothing but tufty moorland to crop.
For now, though, the waiting – December wind numbing bones –
blood thinning – hunger-pangs cramping – nearly out of their minds –
kept going on promises of food...

★

Till nightfall: one of those thin winter skies – open, wide –
a full moon lying deep, almost hugging the horizon, then skimming
the tips of trees – skeletal – and slowly rolling, beginning to climb –
a buttery-colour, huge, haloed with rainbowing hues – and, beneath,
the spread of the hillside, ghostly-white close by, then slicing away
to grey, and black beyond – with a chill wintry wind that shivered
the eerie stillness – sheep barking between nibbles, and huddling
for shelter by shorn hawthorns, the stripped bramble thickets...

★

Moonlight gleaming in eye-beams – amber-red – meant they knew
the ewe's movements, though hadn't reckoned, sight blighted, how keen
her hearing, or fast her scampering, rattling through blackthorns – zag-
zigging through fingers and hands, Dan wrong-footed on tussocks –
slipping, sliding – ewe bleating and blorting – frantic gambolling –
back legs kicking, head bucking – making feints – a stop, then
panicky dashes at flat-out speeds – till Patrick had her jammed fast
between legs, left arm crooked around neck – a raised right, and fall
of his club – thump – again – and the ewe slumped to her knees, rolled
over, blorted, once, with red-black spilling from nostrils and mouth...

Roger Elkin

*

Beneath lamp, Michael did the skinning, slipping her greasy pelt
off like a glove – his knife slicing finely – the ewe's lean frame
pink as a baby, and nearly as thin – and the flat tombstone bloodying
to sacrificial altar. Trussing her crossed ankles with plaited straw,
he slung her over his shoulder, nodded *Go* and, nervous-laughing,
their hearts racing, eyes everywhere, they began their tramping home…

*

Years later, remembering this night – first of many saving them from
hunger, eviction, exile – they blessed those sheep: *All ours for the taking…*

"*If the people are forced to consume their oats and other grain, where is the rent to come from?*"
Captain Perceval, Westport Commissariat Officer, to Charles Edward Trevelyan,
Head of the Treasury, August 14th, 1846 (**Commissariat Correspondence I**, *page 9*)

Dog's Eye View

IV   Blackthorns

Dan and his five Byrne siblings
like so many pavement ravens
had charted them throughout March
in claphatch and trackside:
swags of white stars lagging
along hedgerows, their delicate five petals
stark against the dark thorns.

September was when, young Feargus dead,
the rest of bairns bone-thin, the Byrnes
returned, Dan hoping that chaffinches hadn't
filched the crop – *See, some there. Look. There.*
And there – amidst sprigs of twig, and not yet
fully ripe: sloes, bluish-black and wrapped
in waxy must of greyish bloom.

Taken days before ready, else others
would plunder, they teethed into them,
there and then, cramming mouths with blackness –
whole fruit, hard and firm as pebbles –
that acrid seep from acid-yellow flesh,
till spilling to burst between jammed lips,
juice running glistening down chins,
onto licking fingers; two minutes' greedy eating;
spitting pips; the hard swallowing; the young ones
blarting, stomach griping with aches
of sudden fulness after conacre failures
and days without food.

Some relief.
Hunger pangs numbed, aching sated,
then minds dulled by hedgerows' emptiness:
slow dawning that everyone's tomorrows
had been garnered hastily away.

"Children searched ... the bogs and mountains for berries."
Roger J McHugh, **Food During The Famine***, (1956), page 399*

V   Hunter-Gatherer Dan

Coming home under September sunlight striping
through dawn clouds, Dan trawling his hedgerows
hoping a catch had been sprung in his rabbit-traps,
that the hemp he'd strung across the tell-tale runs
of flattened grass had snagged, and some buck
struggling his anguished freedom-dance had lashed
his last, the strawy-cord tautening around his neck.
But nothing. On nothing. For months. Though found
a grounded crow, its wings dragging the land fanlike –
so cricked its neck, folding beak over feathered breast,
and smudging the dribbling blood with spitty fingers
stuffed its still warm lump under cover of his shirt.

Was when remembered where the mushrooms grew –
stepping-stones pebbling the dewy field, their cream and
brown underskins feeling downy, stems like chalk,
their woody churchyard smell – so stuffed pocketsful.

Then tracking home, flanking Aughamore townland,
past widow Mairin's hut was where, coursing through
the early morning sunlight, saw white slice of raw onion –
half an orb – picking up the sun's shimmering, and
lying face down on the ground below her window.

Silence indoors. And out. No-one save him thereabout.
But left arm gesturing in opposite direction – just in
case – took a swipe with his right foot – then stooped
to scoop – its marble skin slipping, juice sluicing hands –
tucked in with the bird – sniffing fingers the rest of his day.

Showed surprise on hearing how Mairin had gone down
with fever – and dead in less than three weeks – seventy-one –
but never let on where his half-onion had come from.

"If the neighbours suspected there was any fever in the house, they used to steal up to the house at night time and put an onion on the window sill. They would split the onion in two. If the onion turned green they would know that there was fever in that particular house."
Recollection of Richard Delaney, from Cathal Poirtier, **Famine Echoes**, (Dublin, 1995), page 102

Dog's Eye View

VI   *Dan's Dig*

Dan still had his spade, Michael a stolen rope
and Patrick an abandoned net found while trouting
the Shannon, so it was all hopes that no-one else
had visited the earth before them.

Dan had calculated that by digging back to
the backdrop of rock, they'd eventually run out
of runs, tunnels, earthworks, and there'd be
nowhere for escape – *Is when we'll need
that net and rope of yours.*

But hadn't reckoned on the earth depth,
or that, once the top spade-lunge had shifted
soggy clods, the loam was packed that close
Dan could only slice and chip, so the dig became
more exhausting than he'd thought, and what with
the dug soil sliding back on where he'd worked,
and the fact famine rations had sapped his stamina,
before they knew it twilight was threatening,
making the dig a race against time.

Till, suddenly, the ground collapsed – a scrambling –
the lashing of paws – teeth needle-sharp and long –
and eye-patches flashing the face of a highway man
holding self to ransom – trying to back into the back
of itself – to shrink into its own shoulder-blades, but
attack at the same time – head thrashing – wild eyes
glaring – till thrown net – roping round, Michael taking
the strain – a snarling rattle – and it was all over in a flash –
spade raising for a single face-blade – thwack – steel against
flesh – juddering – blood trickle – and a shuddering lump
collapsing into the grey shawl of itself – yellowy claws
stilled now, reduced to fork-tines and trapped beneath
body weight – head lolloping oddly, the shape of a grey log,
and just as lumpish – eyes glazed.

Pleased with themselves, they bundled up the sagging bag
of flesh – *Quick lads* – before its living had been driven
finally to earth, and death caressed its pelt with stiffness.

Theirs at last; one broken trophy:
that has-been of a badger.

"The next morning we ate... a slice of the flesh of fried badger."
M Doheny, **The Felon's Track, or History of the Attempted Outbreak in Ireland Embracing The Leading Events in the Irish Struggle from the Year 1843 to the Close of 1848** *(Dublin edition, 1914), page 260*

Dog's Eye View

VII   *Waiting Game*

It was the smoke-plume and acrid-sweet sniff
of smouldering turf that told Dan the stoking-up
had begun, the makeshift chimney drawing him
just beyond Strokestown's fringe where the stone houses
melted into field edges. There it sat, squatting, ominous
mid-pasture: a hundred gallon boiler almost a carriage-girth,
taking four to maul it into place, the iron-red rust bleeding
through its bitumen black, and its clanging emptiness
dulled as it filled with a mix of water, oats, Indian buck,
onions, turnip, carrots, pease-meal and steeped ox-head
(its tongue long since promised to the Reverend Lloyd).

Loitering at the crowd edge, Dan marvelled where the rest
had magicked from – distant townlanders gathering in knots,
passive as sheep, rag-bags of folk with children wild-eyed
in their thinness – queuing, noggins and cans in hand,
to hear their name called, for bread and soup; and all the time
the officious gaze of Crown Agent Knox, roster in fist,
and the Reverend Lloyd and wife Eleanor smiling benignly.

Patrick McGuire, the carter, wasn't given to waiting, so
parting the crowd like some runaway bull, shoved his way
forward, till confronting Knox head on, demanded *Soup*.
And had it: splashed scalding in his face; spun on heel, and
bolted, hungry-still, cursing *God rot to Hell you English turners*.
The rest might have been stone, standing there, silently ,
waiting in a resignation that made patience a misnomer,
yet came to life once poured their quart of watery prawpeen –
some, driven by hunger, scuttling away to cool their cans
under running springs, others fanning the thin liquid onto planks,
then, on all fours, lapping catlike through their blistered lips.

Roger Elkin

As for Dan, he'd learnt to manage his famine pangs, so hung
lagging back, knowing from what he'd been told over poteen
at driver Cox's shebeen that the best would rest on the pot's bottom –
and the finest, the screb-crust, left to be picked off, its crackly patches
scratching tongue, and fingers glistening with dribbled fat and spit.
Later Dan japed with the Reillys *Sure, 'tis written in the Scriptures:
To him who asks will it be given – or so Carter McGuire knows!*

"The food best suited for free relief is soup."
Government circular to the Secretary of Relief Committees in Ireland,
January 20^h, 1847

Dog's Eye View

VIII   Stinging Proddys

Putting Strokestown's tree-lined street behind them,
Dan and the Reilly lads, billhooks and flax-rag in hands,
struck out for St John's, the Mahon church, Dan averring –
Even a Proddy God will provide – though crossed himself
like the others, then took turn rolling over the graveyard wall,
to stay waiting, safe behind headstones, breath held in a mix
of suspicion-guilt become penance-confessional.

Not sure if Reverend Lloyd was out calling, they zag-tracked
the yew colonnade, and at woodpigeon-rattle through branches
tried vanishing into trees, burying themselves bolt up against
centuries of feathery leaf in bluish-black-green with shadows
lit by scarlet berries, hard and inviting. *Theys Lucifer's blood –*
Michael jibed, schooled with the other townland kids not to eat
by Father Geraghty – *Will whip you boys straight down to Hell.*

Once out into the clearing, their prize was sighted: regiments
of angular stems, nearly three feet tall, hanging with flags of leaves,
and dressed in tresses of yellowing seeds as gritty as last season's
salmon roe. *See whys we needed our flax-rag* – and Dan had a bunch
of strands tightly grasped in his left hand, while his right slashed
in arcs of light, the billhook slicing through wiry veins, leaving sap
weeping anaemically. The other two grinned at Dan's quipping –
There's nothing stopping us cropping the alls of them.

Twenty minutes of frantic hacking – frond-piles divided equally –
life draining out of teethed leaves curling under the sun. Then
all the time taking care to keep hands, arms, legs clear – quick
bandaging with flax – to carry home, feeling bolder now, knowing
cabins would clatter with the flash of knives on table and bench,
the leaves macerated to dark green seeps, then mixed with soaked oats
for stouping into week-long soup. Patrick it was had the last words –
Better than starving, this stinging Proddys. And with God's own weeds.

"I heard my own mother to say she saw the people travelling miles to the graveyards to gather the nettles... They grew higher and better in graveyards than any other where."
Irish Folklore Commission, Cork Archive, ii 10

IX   Pallbearers

O'Connor it was who told Dan – *Padraig has passed*;
but the donkey long gone for food and their cart bartered,
it came down to carrying – and, before the lads knew it, they
were wresting planks from the back of Padraig's dresser,
and, placing them as makeshift bench, their mouths gagged
with rag, they bent over his fever-wracked corpse, swagged
its sagging weightlessness like a sack of praties, swung it up,
and bumped it, laying straight, on the board. Dan plaited
his straw round Padraig's ankles, while Michael tied down
the head, fined back almost to bone, and Patrick steadied
the lamp's nervy rhythmic swinging. *Is lift, we have, lads.*

And then the slow lurch and stumble to the church –
five miles – through the night, the three of them taking turns –
two shouldering, one either end, the third carrying lamp
and picking out the coffin-tracks till they reached St John's.

Scanlan and Gaughan, guarding the graveyard against
marauders, sent them down to where mounds of fresh-dug clay
defined the Famine pit. Turning the lamp so its beams pierced
the gloom of the twelve-foot depth, Dan scanned the pile
of bodies, and amid the mix of limbs and swollen forms
picked out the shape of six faces and heads. He blenched, then
retched at the rising stench. Once more standing tall, he gave
the pre-agreed head-signal, and Michael and Patrick, slipping off
the knotted straw, angled the plank, and slid Padraig – *Amen Amen* –
bump-thudding down the hole's darkness to the giving squelch.

Feelings numbed and coffin-pence clutched in sticky palms,
they picked the five miles back home in silence. Once safe,
they stored the plank in Dan's roof. Was several days before
shoulders lost their ache and tongues took up rationalities again.

"*They dug graves 12 foot deep and put seven or eight bodies into each grave. They never put coffins on them at all. Some of the bodies used to swell up and when they would be dropped in to the grave they would burst.*"

John Doyle, Rasheenmore, **Irish Folklore Commission** *1075: 200*

Dog's Eye View

X   Dan Views The Atlantic

Almost an hour's loading that December morning,
lamps guttering in the chilling wind; the gangmaster
cracking whip; cows, bullocks – square Irish blacks –
barely visible through the dark apart from the beams
of light trapped by their amber eyes in the rhythmic
river-surge, heads, rumps, flanks rising and falling,
hooves clacking on gangplanks and skittering in shit,
cattle sashaying, all the time shoving and being shoved
into the steerage hold, steam and breath spiralling...

While standing, passive, silent at Sligo dockside, nigh on
two hundred famine passengers waiting to board. And Dan
among them. How he'd landed here, he'd no idea, but
since the Riley lads had been lost to fever, he'd been
anchorless. So drifted west. Thought it was Liverpool
not London he was heading for, so couldn't understand
why **Londonderry** was limed across the steamer's prow.

Once on board, all anticipation, underscored by the engine's
thrumming, the steamer slipping clear of Drumcliff Bay
with Sligo cupped in the inlet behind, the 8a.m. December sun,
thin and milky, casting pale angles between clouds and
bathing the pewter sea in light. Not having been twenty miles
beyond his Doorty townland, Dan hadn't seen such vast
expanse of water, so the Shannon and Lough Ree dwindled into
insignificance against the tumbling Atlantic's grey-brown reach.
Behind him, huge slabs of rock as if they'd been lifted and
slapped down at all angles – Slieve League – some strata vertical,
others pulled as if the rock were slurry – the Cliffs of Bunglass –
like slices of cattle-hide, stretched, unrumpled. And Dan,
transfixed, humbled by the surge and boil of the Atlantic
where his and millions others New Edens would begin.

"At 8 a.m. on Friday 1 December 1848, the steamer **Londonderry** *left Sligo for Liverpool with a cargo of passengers and cattle... Two days later she arrived at Liverpool with 72 of her 174 passengers dead."*
*Moving Here: **Migration Histories**: www.movinghere.org.uk.* **Tragedy at Sea**

One of those passengers may have been Dan.

Roger Elkin

HUNTING WILD

African-eyed like sad cows
he has left Morocco.
There are no date palms in London,
no camels bearing loads,
and flies are not so busy here.

Though hashish is bartered
in back street deals, alcohol freely spills
and women wear faces in public:
he cannot unhook his looks
from their lips.

Westernized, he grows rings
on his wedding finger.
But, at night, dreams of the friendship of lads,
white midday suns, opaline skies
and cool winds freshening over dunes.

In this new Mecca
though he has relinquished the old gods,
how he misses the call
of the muezzin in the minaret.
He cannot stop his gaze turning
to the East.

Innocent as his olive skin,
he is not old enough to understand
societies have separate addictions,
or that Truth slides and wrinkles
like youthful looks.

For the now, he knows these absolutes:
the arrogance of loneliness,
the openness of need.

Dog's Eye View

OF PERFECTION

The Nubian bar-staff – lads to a man –
stand behind their maroon and tan uniforms
and eye up and down the frauleins, mademoiselles,
the English girls.

Never so much female flesh seen before this season:
sheer perfection.

How their eyes climb glaciers of backs,
            abseil cliffs of shoulders,
            chasm down cleavages,
            slide past temples of plenty,
                tombs of wombs,
then drop anchor at pubic deltas:
sheer perfection.

And how – the whites of their eyes already yellowing –
they save their face behind practised smiles
as wide as the Nile

then melt away
to the store-room behind the bar
where, getting a grip on things,
they begin to bring themselves to perfection.

(Aswan, Egypt)

LOOSFERS CHIL
(after the painting 'The Hunted Slaves' by Richard Ansdell)
for Gladys Mary Coles

Dey col mi blek bast'd, elloun, darki,
Loosfers chil, big brut, laz-ee dawg
Dey be ful of nems dat urt

Man, dey kik mi, dey beet, dey thrash,
Wipanlash – yeh, dey urt mi mad
Dey lyk ter see de culler o mah blud,
Lyk de smel o mah blud, lyk mah owlin

Dey col mi shit, dey kik de shit outta mi,
Feed mi shit, leaf mi lyin derr in shit,
But dey shit, man, dey shit

Dey chen mi tite til de blud run
Dey shu njoy mah suffrin, wik mi in gans,
Le mi boil in de sun, nah drin de day lon,
Nah res, wikin de day lon, and wen ren cum
Dey kip mi oudoors awl nigh lon, in de dar

Dey gonna kil mi sumday

Dey tuk awey mah libatee
Dey not nis man
Col mi blek trash, it mi, wip mi,
Kip mi from mah famlee, mah sons, mah dams,
Don le mi secks

Dees bos man, dey nah Crisjuns
Ain nuthin nis abaht dem
Dey awl de sem

Dey dun ron doin awl dis bad ter mi
So ahm goin fur freedm
Gettin mah owhn bek, goin fur dem

Dats mi, derr in de picher,
De darki on de lef

Dog's Eye View

Richard Ansdell: The Hunted Slaves XIX Century

Jan van Eyck (1387) – (1441): Untitled, known in English as The Arnolfini Portrait,
The Arnolfini Wedding, The Arnolfini Marriage, The Arnolfini Double Portrait, or
Portrait of Giovanni Arnolfini and his Wife,
The Marriage of Giovanni Arnolfini and Giovanna Cenami

ARNOLFINI VARIATIONS
based on Jan van Eyck's:
The Marriage of Giovanni Arnolfini and Giovanna Cenami

I *A Wedding Portrait*
i.m. *Charles Causley*

Young man, young woman gazing down
praise painter's skill for drawing eyes
not first to note your union
of flesh, but his reflected face
placed boldly at the picture's focal
point, and, just above (almost like
some travelled Kilroy-signature
but penned in showy Gothic scrawl)
his witness: *Johannes de eyck fuit hic. 1434.*

Once seen, Giovanni, right hand
vertical like the risen Christ's,
seems too straight-laced, expression bland,
face glum, eyes quenched. Close by his waist
fingers extend to touch his bride –
not firmly clenched, but hand in palm –
as he intones his bond to her.
Broad-brimmed hat, oddly worn inside,
looks haloish; his bearing's calm,
proud, secure; grey cloak limned with fur.

Giovanna, in love's shade, green,
left hand on paunch, face Virginal
and meek, stands silently, her mien
pure as she accepts her bridal
state. Eyes scan the floor. Her rich gown
with snaking trim and pleated folds
distracts the gaze from her full womb
where breeds their need's consummation.
Denying all that marriage holds
unique, her quick form's their lust's tomb.

To illustrate their piety
they must have paid this artist well
for, near the glass, her rosary
hangs down; while mirror's roundels tell
Christ's via crucis; and the carved
chairback frames St Margaret's tale. Note,
though, he hints *their* death: the griffin
terrier at their feet seems some suave
knight's tomb-dog, with, on high, one lit
candle for a votive offering.

Symbolic perspectives apart,
the detail depicts the tenor
of their times. But, though citrus fruit
ripening for use to bring labour
on, his near bed, their scattered shoes
suggest the haste to fix love's vows
before *her* day, such niceties
as sin and shame van Eyck reviews
by having portraiture espouse
fidelities in art, and eyes.

Dog's Eye View

II *A Dog's Eye View*
i.m. U A Fanthorpe

Took a dog's day snapping at heels, scratching at doors,
nearly wagging my tail off to get in on this. Though I traded
three good-dogs, Master didn't want me included, but Yan-man,
smelling of linseed and with streakmeat smock, insisted – see
him reflected in the background – though he even left me off
till just before he cleaned out his brushes on the wall. That's
why I'm walks-now up to him. The she-man standing in the door
has whined two sunfuls about nothing but confinement. Suppose
it means no going here-boy all today. Again. She keeps turning
to sunlight the new fetch-boys she's brought in. Why won't she
seek-out with me? Master's not himself either. He's not usually
so serious and pale, but there have been growlings long into
the fire with the grey old ones who clean behind my ears and
updown with sit-begs; and now he's wearing Sunday clothes
and hat, even though it's a selling-day, and he's indoors.

I blame that other she-man. Since she came here, there's all
those gnawbones littering the floor, or pushed just under
the day-couch. Then by the see-self on the wall there's the gristly
string she walks her fingers on while she talks to herself. Once
I could heel-boy and seek-out her eyes, but something's come
between us. Now I have to stand a walk-away to see her face.

I used to be Master's lap; but now she's the one that has him
rough-and-tumbling, though you wouldn't know today. He isn't
even good-boys with her, doesn't walk-smile; and his voice is
like the big black book he speaks aloud each day. She's not sit-stay
for long, but throw-fetched, then stretched her length on the day-couch.
If she's got that after-eat-now feel, the big lie-down's close at hand.

To make things worse, there's woof of coming child. Hope it isn't
Master's brother's brat who pulls, prods and two-legs me, then yelps
when I nip, and mouth-wides when they bang me like the rug. Couldn't
stand that today. Though Yan-man's got a wag-tail likeness, it isn't
worth getting famous to be framed by kids. Oh, Dog forbid.

Roger Elkin

COMING CLEAR
For Mary

Time was when, though you saw the art,
you might have blenched. But when
the man in brown, the gallery's man, paid
by State to protect the art, declared *The man is bent*
you leapt to distant Hockney's defense.

Don't you see the pictures as part of a plan,
a sequence making a modern Rake's Progress,
Hockney out-Hogarthing Hogarth, bringing it up to date.
To see them singly is to miss the point. There's the artist,
see him going for a plane. That man with the third round eye's
the psychiatrist, and there's the artist, coffined up
in Bedlam. That's what we've done to art:
declared it mad, because it's near the bone.

Then further on *What we've got in those clean-lined limbs,*
those two men lying in bed, asleep; one getting dressed;
or washed; or getting up – isn't rape or lust,
child-battering, but love. Man living with man.
See how the lines are clean; there's no eroticism.

You mean he's queer.

No, homosexual. Love's everyone's worth;
and being loved doesn't corrupt, or hurt, or kill.

He's queer as well as bent! the brown man huffed.

You didn't take the bait. At times words no longer help;
silence becomes the best contempt.

Like art, like love, like life, it takes time to connect
and sometimes connecting lines are brown, or bent, or queer.
One day, perhaps, it'll all come clear:
those clean-lined limbs, guardianed by the State,
progressed beyond a sneer, and hung upon a wall
for all to comprehend in clean-lined minds.

Dog's Eye View

MASQUES
i.m. John Ogden

Szymanowski's filigree fills the hall
notes dappling the darkness   rhythms stirring the stillness
themes breathing   ebbing and rising
nudging at wall corners   feeling the ceiling   lapping at doors
laving carpets   absorbing curtains   handling drapes
searching the listeners   finding their minds   their chests
fingering their blood   their bones   back to the backs of their seats
numbing their limbs   their hands   pinning them to silence

At centre sealing their attention, a meal of a man, alone
upstaged by a vaster piano anvil. He's tied to it, forging
his being, firing a living. Hands pounding from piano to head,
huge fingers dripping over slipping keys, finger-ends nailing
his mind to the keyboard.
The keys are kneading, a sort of resuscitation.
The music is lifting   is soaring   till he's dragging
himself from memory's recesses, reining it,
holding it deep within him   deep down within him
the wedge-hands reforming him
piecing together those crotchets and quavers   those bar marks
and time schemes   making a meaning from the acne of dots
and the spaces between.
And he's coming out again   being made again
delivering himself with his own hands   into his own hands
his own resurrection.

It is finished.

Silence grinds a relief. The crowd
finds hands again. Applause water-
falls

Bemused with a new self, he's all smiles

Memory edges a necessary bow; he searches the foolish floor
and abandoning the piano to blackness
ambles away, the asylum's Caliban.

John Ogden emerged from a mental hospital on 5th February 1981 to give a recital at the Queen Elizabeth Hall. It was his first public performance in four years.

Roger Elkin

CLASSIFIER
For Judy Seago

Organizing authors in some logical order, she sits,
Undeterred by name or fame, behind her island issue-desk;
Rules – by franking-stamp, dates of return and reading-lists –

Life's waywardness. Fortified by stacks of books
Is never at a loss for words: holds them all at fingertips;
Borrows titles, names as others might pick up their friends;
Reads lenders sooner than they can their choice; keeps
Autobiographies of them from the tomes they request; lends
Romance to uglies, pipe-dreams to plumbers, and feeds aspiring poets
Inspired diets of Heaney, Larkin, Causley, Hughes.
Arching brows over ice-grey eyes bring silences. (She believes it's
Nonsense using words where decimal points confuse.)

Is a masterly, mystic wizard with most classification:
Seldom resorts to reference. Knows that in Dewey's system

Jung slips unconsciously between Philosophy and Sociology;
Understands that while Semantics find meaning in Linguistics,
Dictionaries might list themselves in columns alphabetically,
Yoga must be positioned between Religion and Gymnastics.

She considers (though others may view them with some mystery)
English Miracles are not tricks, just Literature; she might fix
Alchemy dramatically as fiction, but occasionally permits
Geography to travel adventuring in realms of History.
Only Love's a problem. Is it Field Sports? Engineering?
                    Or maybe Chemistry?

Or all of those? Or Poetry? Even Congress leaves the choice unsolved.
Knowledge of self's an issue she's never classified, franked or shelved.

Dog's Eye View

STORY TELLING
i.m. Peter Copson

O Henry's book in hand, firm anchorage for nerves,
words falling precisely but with quiet compassion,
mouth reining back images, you unwrapped
a tale of Christmas gifts, which once swapped
would prove the depth of partner's love.

You told how each gave up for other what was precious:
Jim, gold fob-watch to dress her hair in set of tortoise-comb;
Della, cascading hair to buy for him watch-chain of platinum.
With gifts neither ornament or use, both felt impoverished,
forgetting that they had their love.

At end, startled by the sudden raw applause
that broke the spell created by your voice,
your eyes eloquent with sympathies,
fell, and closed.

Your wife, installed behind the piano, and hidden from your sight,
spilled wet stars onto the silent keyboard.

By sharing of yourselves in deed and speech,
O Henry's tale was thus resolved: and all enriched,
as on a chain of words there hung a strand of falling tears.

Roger Elkin

ETYMOLOGIES

Going through the gate   *gat*, Old Norse – opening
along the slow, winding path   *pad*, Middle Low German – path
past the pagodas of nettles   *pagode*, Portuguese – temple
the squinting scarlet pimpernels *saqalat*, Persian – rich vermilion cloth
flanking Collier's garden   *gart*, Old High German – enclosure
with its laughing daffodils   *de affodil*, Dutch – asphodel
its harlot tulips   *tulbend*, Turkish – turban

and strolling down to the allotment   *hlot*,   Old English – lot
with its straight rows of potatoes   *batata*, Spanish – potato
parading cabbages   *caboche*, Middle English – head
spritting broccoli crop   *broccolo*, Italian – small nail
regiment of feathery carrots   *carrotte*, Middle French — carrot
the gone-to-seed rhubarb
with its assegai flower-spears   *az-zaghaya*, Arabian – iron-tipped spear

and in the distance
the wooden holiday bungalow   *bangla*, Hindi – house in Bengal style
straddled by panelled-glass veranda   Hindi – gallery

across the yard, a garden shed
reeking of creosote   *kreas*, Greek – oily flesh
where was brought to orgasm   *orgasmos*, Greek – organ, growing ripe

a singular practice, revisited since, many times
in both classical and spiritual mode
as   masturbation   *masturbari*, Latin – to masturbate
          self-abuse   *abuti*, Latin – to use away
          onanism   after Onan, **Genesis**, 38, 9 – seed-spiller

and subsequently buggered up   *bougre*, Middle French – commit heresy
to learn the origin of wanking   in popular use – that done by wankers
isn't Anglo-Saxon, after all
but taboo in several dictionaries   *tabu*, Tongan – unclean
and always much closer to hand   vulgar, possibly 20th Century American

SPOOKY PODMORE

Outsider to our lads' gang, you moped silently
on the edge of things, or suddenly loomed –
a mooning *Three Stooges'* ghoul – dead-eyed,
long armed, swooping frame, white formed – that sent
shivers goosepimpling through our skinny limbs.

Somehow alien, it was your quietness that spoke you;
and your looks that spawned your nickname:
that pale flat disc of face with its stare
almost piercing backwards through your head
and making you barn-owlish – not in the wise old way,
but primitive, frightening, glaring – as if you
could tear us to pieces and pellet us out:
spookish... and spooked... spooky...

Four decades later, seeing you by chance
in your block-paved drive as you worship-wash
your white Mercedes Benz, with, behind you,
your three-bed bungalow – detached – full *upvc*,
double-glazed and fashionable gravel path –
you're still owlish: wide-eyed but strangely blank
and glassy; a beaky nose; and mechanical bird-twist
of head: cross between can't-touch-me-separateness
and arrogance born of that down-class ambition –
and still that spooky cool allure...

Yes, got to admit, you're streets away, in all senses,
from that Uplands council-house with red-raddled steps
and the pebble-dash of fifties England. Certainly have spooked
me now with your distant edge, your quiet remove...

But suddenly my mind becomes flooded by memories
of that snatched glance of you – not yet in trousers –
jerking off Latham's dog in silent fervour:
Aagh, the grisly pink of that slicked dick...
and you're reduced to Spooky Podmore once more...
pelleted remnant...

But then, I guess you always were a wanker...

Roger Elkin

THE TROUBLE WITH BEING A W

"Candidates whose surnames commence with letters from the second half
of the alphabet are at a distinct disadvantage"
Report on a More Egalitarian System for the Interviewing Procedure

I suppose initially I have problems with identity:
I even wonder at myself. Am I a What? A Which? Or a merely Who?
Perhaps I'm schizoid; I fear I'm really split apart in two.
In mirrors I glimpse a wraith ghosting me indefinitely.

I have troubles too with place, and occasionally time.
You've guessed? Where, Whither and then When. It's true
I'm not quite the centre of anywhere, and, despite wisdom,
Always the final in the row. No wonder I haven't got a clue.

Is it, you think, I'm wanting in initiative? Yes, I am a sheep,
Even, at heart, a ewe. Where others lead, I always follow,
And though I start work strongly at the beginning of the week
I am so weakened by the weekend I'm through.

I'm in a double-act, but never know who pulls the string
In me, or who's ventriloquist. I'm somebody's fallguy too,
The butt of everyone's whim. And when I get it wrong
I fall so silent that I'm overlooked. I'm in nobody's queue.

I'm also missing out in sex. I've a headstart with wooing wenches,
But fear I'm wishy-washy, transparent as a window, seen clear through
From beginning to end. And (just between we two) I never arrive in climaxes.
Suppose I'm the wo(e) in woman. Or am I losing a screw, or maybe two?

Though I appear boldly in World Wars, I'm never mentioned
In dispatches. I miss the boat, and nearly miss the show.
And because of names like Janowitz, Johannsen, not to mention Jung
Am practically always last one in at the interview.

This döppelganger in my name is weird for me. I wish I were a singleton,
But then suppose I'd worry that the other one, the simpler man,
Were my better half. Oh how I wish I wasn't what I am.
Don't scoff; be glad it's me, not you, that's neither U nor yet non-U
But just a puddled, fuddled, muddled, troubled W.

CHRYSANTHEMUM JIM

Something there is stubbed and stopped about him
like his specimens. His fingers are as thick as stems
and hands like spades from when his father had the farm
and work *was* work, at labourings of forty loads a day
for eight and six a week. Recalling greenhouses, his face
grows into smiles. He lists a catechism: the eight by ten;
the twenty-one by twelve; the forty foot whose roof they
spragged when putting in new sides. Though reduced
to three cold frames and potting shed, this September sees
him, carpet-slipper-clad, steeped shoulder-high in parades
of paper bags that shield his flowers from frosts and rain.

Nowadays he gives most of them away, yet persists
all year with cuttings, stools and buds – a lifetime's ritual
that counterpoints the residues of Autumn shows he's
shelved indoors (coloured cards in fancy script, medals,
tarnished cups) from when he swept the North in City Halls
with incurved globes as big as bowls. Confirmed misogynist
he unashamedly confides he knows
no woman half as good as most his blooms;
can't recognize betrayals in their names – Edna Rowes,
Eve Grays, Ginger Nuts, Old Flames – nor admit as passion
the way he fondles stems, caresses leaves, makes eyes
at buds. Approaching eighty, he's prey to philosophy –
You spend a lifetime, then it's done and gone.
Like this – and snags a flower head, whose petals
feather down in silent martyrdom.

THAT COMMITTEE MEMBER

is bereft of pity.

Eyes seem soft as a doe, –
but are mean like a hawk's.
He strikes where he likes:
lets no weakness slips his gaze.

Hands birdish, his fingers circle and wheel,
take time to settle on meaning.

Cobra-laconic
he tortures attention,
his words slow as lazing snakes
in waiting
or quick-flicking lizard-twitchy
in picking off victims.

Is lean as a weasel.

Expect he frigs like a pig.

Is so much an animal
best make a monkey of him
elect him Minute secretary.

Dog's Eye View

BIG SISTER'S FORMER BOYFRIENDS

You know, that loose gang of gaggly lads
that hung around our back gate, or sat
thin-bummed on the front wall ledged
between railing stumps cut down
for the war effort, those lads in jitterbug shoes,
drainpipe slacks, crew cuts –
all bravado and cup-handed smokers:

"Presley" Smith, the Elvis of the town
with his blue suede shoes and moody looks;
Cedric with his sudden carrot-red;
Ray and his eight-inch dick (or so
my sister whispered to me one night, her eyes
widening and fingers spanning into light);
or Jim who passed me scrappy notes
for her with SWALK scrawled raungily
in black Quink ink; and Geoff who leant
on doorjambs asking Mum in practised
nonchalance if Mags was coming out.

Seeing them twenty years on –
"Presley" hush-puppying round dance halls
in smooching croons or trying since his baby
left him to grind some square tango round;
Cedric with his ratting-cap; Ray sporting
lump-pushing cords; Jim ground down with
his postman's round; and Geoff the joiner
with nicotined hands – helps me understand
why she picked the lad with Pat Boone teeth
and fresh American looks, who never smoked
and had all things in proportion.

Roger Elkin

True, he's spawned a gut and has perhaps
more hair (combed forward), not to mention
bungalow, two kids, two cars, and though
he suffers from vertigo (too much worrying
over his bank balance?) he still has all his teeth.
(Our Mags keeps hers all night
grinning acidly in a glass.)

Seeing them, seeing her, seeing him
I cringe at how I might have become to them
that soft prick of a milk-tooth kid now lead sexophone
in Lonely Street's Heartbreak Hotel.

Dog's Eye View

SALES REP

Risen King of the Waxing Year,
his mastery of the Golden Fleece
is fast making him a living myth.
Since almost all he touches turns to sold
he's betrayed the old God of Protestant thrift
and embraces the Profit Margin
with its Trinity of the ashtray, the in-tray, the out-tray.
In the Word Processor is his beginning,
and his end the printout listing his Ascension.
His catechism is the daily calculating of cash.

He has bought off his class handicaps:
sold the best part of his life to the Woolwich;
his wife to the certainty of infidelity;
his soul to twenty years' indemnity.
Because he knows that climbing higher
becomes lonelier-colder, has acquired accents
cruel as crampons, yet feels assured that his falling voice
will abseil him to safety.
Reckoning others by cars, estimates his value as a BMW:
drives himself hard.
His politics are arrival, and greed.

Though most times would agree with Plato
that Poets are at best excluded,
he evokes the Muse to cast advertising runes,
and envies Shakespeare's felicity with words.
Unschooled in the Classics,
has eclipsed the principles of Euclid
with a multiplication as rabid as dandelions.
He magpies Latin tags *ad nauseam*;
to compensate for absence of uniform
has tallboys of old school ties.
His address book is a Yellow Pages;
left hand a Visa card; right one mobile phone.
He measures success by the length of his lunch-break;
and his taste by the bitter he pisses.
He bleeds cheap red wine.

Roger Elkin

Monogrammed briefcase and cufflinks
are the depository of his being;
he folds his id away in a travelling hangrobe;
keeps his shadow at bay by a battery buzz.

In his vocabulary there's no room for sweat:
Old Spice breeds in his crotch;
in his armpit lurk Pagan and Brut.

Has sold success to himself
by selling the animal in himself:
uses hands like fangs; is dog-lazy, and sudden;
picks ideas off like toads lashing flies;
unstares folk to the bone;
adopts clothes like a chameleon.
And when he fucks, fucks like a ferret –
mouth on their nape: *Quick – Now – Quick – Quick –*
his eyes wide open, fixed on the sex axis,
his why axis those figures and curves,
discharging sperm like largesse.

SEPTEMBER SUNDAY

One of those days, wide-eyed, full-faced,
when looking becomes squinnying
and everything narrows to thins,
horizon-bladed, confined.

Have to get out.

The light is liquid bright: almost thin;
and the sky wide open, and birds
in their bobbing flight like flies
trying to get through glass, cannot get
out: there's no window to open.

The clean-lined hedges,
the angles of stone-walls playing
marquetry with the moor;
every piece in place so though
gates are gaping there is nothing
through which to escape.

Saplings are like thin cuts
in the sky's clean face:
if they were pulled open,
wider from the inside
there'd be a way out.
But they cannot begin.

That way today would be
a walk-through.
Apart from memory there's nothing
of you; and though it extends
a hand, it lacks warm touch, firm grip
to pull it all fully through.

So cannot get out there.

So sharing is internal;
is partial; is not at all.

Wish you were here.

Roger Elkin

ORDERS OF THE GARTER

Not those dark blue ribbons, edged
with gold and *Honi soit qui mal y pense*
picked out around some aristocrat's left leg:
always so princely old, or fat,
with ribanded sash that cuts indulgent tums
diagonally in half. If I were damsel in distress,
I wouldn't want whisking off by flatulent dragons
such as this. Where I'm concerned, knights
should have monopolies of youth. Pity Edward III
didn't keep his court affairs in camera; and
Countess Salisbury a tighter grip on things.

Not those fancy bands, ruched in pleats
of scarlets, golds or pinks, with rosettes
flowering up thighs of tarts in slitted
skirts. (With older women it's alabasters
of flabby skin that somehow smacks of abattoirs.)
Not really meant to keep a stocking up – placed
low enough to catch the eyes, and high
enough to tantalize – more designed for
taking down. Odd, though, how Aunt Lil,
in many ways so practical, should spend
her evening hours in circling silks
for no one save her family to view.

No, not these grandiose designs – but
the common or garden things for kids:
those mangy thins, with just a bit
of give, that held long socks in place,
and itched both legs. They were never
meant for public view, but only seen
rolled down for indoor gym, revealing
legends of propriety imprinted in white
on red, while on the bench they twitched
to figure eights. There's no knightliness,
or sex, within a greying garter – just
collapsing sadness like old age.

ONCE SNOOKERED, TWICE...

She catches his eyes,
    blue as her denim-blue skirt, and smiling coyly
    in an inviting boyish tease – that mirror-rehearsed
    don't-daring-then-staring manner – then turning
    and posing to comb, once again, his sleek-creamed
    hair, flicking his front quiff and streamlining sides
    to the D A shape at his nape; invites with his eyes...

reads his lips,
    his teeth slicking and rolling the carmine skin
    glistening with spit till the fulness pleat
    of his girlish pout (the sort his film-heroes sport),
    melts into a winning grin. No spoken words, but
    Bin snookered he mouths, tongue flicking redly...

fancies his form
    Snookered he grizzles aloud to himself, then circles
    the billiard table, eyes shining widely, lips pouting.
    Stops dead. Is certain. Bends knees, squats, and heels
    uplifted, leans meanly, his eyes at baize level, calculates
    angles, till upright once more. Chalks twice his
    cue-tip – slice, slice – and right leg anchored, left
    lying aslant the cushion, his left fingers arching into
    bridge, right stroking the cue – quivering the length –
    forward, back, forward – stretches self to limits of burst...

(her eyes rise from his shoe, through calf to lean thigh,
trace the give and strain, the play of his splayed muscles,
that rippling slide, and up to his tight bum and that revealed
sneak of crotch...)

    and smack: the ball drives home: rattles through angles,
    passes at a fraction, and he shrills *Still snookered Shite*...

and later,
>how they come to be here at Tin Bridge, she just
>doesn't know, though now knows his name – *Lester
>like jockey Not city* – as he pushes her hard against
>bricks, his mouth eight-circling hers, curled tongue
>forcing teeth to French kissing, his dick stiffening
>aside her thigh and, eyes widening, he's trying to unclasp
>her bra (handsful more than Anne's knots-on-cotton).
>By instinct fired on desire, her hands are magnetized
>to his fly; fumble Y-fronts; glide down groin and stop
>short at fuzz of hair. She's on cue: strokes the tip-end,
>and arching fingers – forward, back, forward – quivering
>the length, herself all under wetness brings him to the limits
>of burst
>*Jeesaz Mairy Never bin 'effin snookered before...*

almost forty years after,
>re-sees him at a Tesco's less-than-ten checkout,
>face flaccidly passive, lips given up on kissing,
>dulled hair combed flatter and streaked in snaking grey,
>and eyes still stark blue, but older, colder:
>no daring, but just vacant staring
>and no recognition of how that night he'd slipped
>so quickly through those ready fingers...

is relieved
>but not snookered for life...

Dog's Eye View

VALENTINO'S AQUACLASSES FOR WOMEN OF MIXED NATIONALITY

Twelve of them (most old enough to be his grandma)
lend themselves daily at ten to the pool's chill thrill.
Here the Italian slip of a lad pits them to fitness
under the Greek sun's holiday eye: they're saving their youth.

   ein zwei drei vier fünf sechs sieben acht

Mye bu-tee-full wiman he shrills from the water,
cam to mee. His glistening figure jigs to the music's
racing bass – slipping slapping flipping flapping clapping hands –
as he restirs the youth in their limbs.

   un deux trois quatre cinque six sept huit

They're locked to his shock of cropped black hair, his knifing smile
as he stretches them – in out / up down / forward back.
His thin eyes pin them. He's limber; they lumber.

   one two three four five six seven eight

Nut-brown, neat-limbed, flat chested, balletic: he's blade of a youth.
They're veritable feasts: melon-breasted, white thighs of Gorgonzola folds,
hams of arms, and heads hennaed and permed
more than the hue and curl of their youth.

   uno due tre quatro cinque sei sette otto

By day, they love him like their sons, ride his jibes, feign dismay;
but, at night in the silent films of their dreams see their own
Valentinos rudolfing in silk, stretching wide their thighs – in out in.

He, by day, stretches mind to refind them forty years past:
clean-lined, trim-fit as beauty queens, lissome as him;
and at night, saved by the drained pool, he slips between
his lover's silk sheets and the rhythm of keeping his youth.

   sei six sei six sei sechs

   say *sex sex sex sex*

   say *sex*

LANGUAGE CLASSES

When you have tried
a variety of evening greetings

       Greek: kalaspera
       Romanian: buona serra
       Serbian: dobra vece

and the waiting staff
still curry favour
with the German girls

               Guten Abend

then you understand
the language of age

               Good Night.

Dog's Eye View

Roger Elkin has reviewed for *Stand, Outposts, Envoi;* and is Poetry Tutor on residential weekend courses at Wedgwood Memorial College, Barlaston: for full details see: http://www.stoke.gov.uk/wedgwoodmemorialcollege

He became the first recipient of the Howard Sergeant Memorial Award for Services to Poetry in 1987. His poetry has received the Lake Aske Memorial Award (1982 & 1987), the Douglas Gibson Memorial Award (1986) the Sylvia Plath Award for Poems about Women (1986) and the Hugh MacDiarmid Trophy (2003). He was editor of *Envoi* for fifteen years.

CRITICAL RESPONSES TO ROGER ELKIN'S POEMS

Points of Reference

"Skilful and erudite... The language is sharp and observational, and succeeds in raising the quotidian to poetic realms... The final section of the book, reflecting the poet's visit to Istria.... is a dark, worthy portrayal of a people struggling against poverty and the greed of capitalism which threatens to destroy the traditional way of life."

Chapman

"Roger Elkin's poems are crafted and disciplined. In France... a touch of homesickness is countered by the delights of exploring another culture and... in Istria (former Yugoslavia) the plum must of slivovitz kicks in and the poems successfully concentrate on the resilience of the people."

Emma Hooper, *Poetry Quarterly Review*

Home Ground

"All Elkin's talents, his careful observation, his precision, his unobtrusive delicate craftsmanship, his subtle manipulation of language, go into these fine poems... There are no fireworks, no attitudinising, no writing-for-effect, just the genuine spur of commitment to the subject and the working-out of this passion in language and image. He is not afraid to feel, either... There's no lack of descriptive flair, but Elkin's work offers far more than the superficial... Not many people can write good nature poetry: Elkin can. *Home Ground*, leisurely, humane, committed, is a rich and rewarding corrective for those whose hearts might sink at the prospect."

J G Collingwood, *Envoi*

"As one swims in the sea of poems appearing in magazines and collections, one comes across many that are good but in a minor way; poems based on snippets of autobiography, domestic incidents and a little philosophising, in which the language is ordinary. So one applauds loudly when one comes across a collection

Roger Elkin

which is more than that, where the subject matter is hard and strong and where there is vigour, originality and a strong pulse in the words."

W H Petty, *Acumen*

Rites of Passing

"Sure to enhance Elkin's reputation as a poet of sinewy, meditative power."

John Lucas

"Honest, unpretentious, and crafted with the skill of long apprenticeship in the vineyards where the good red grows... As possessed by death as Webster, ... but transformed into something positive by habitual seriousness, thoughtfulness, and an energy which refuses to lie down."

Eddie Wainwright

Blood Brothers: New & Selected Poems

"A very impressive collection with a large number of well crafted poems... Elkin can build up a poem with a huge resource of skill, employing a seemingly endless catalogue of observation and anecdote. He has a real sense of structure, almost like a novelist's. Each detail, idiosyncrasy and conversation is placed to maximum effect... revealing a potent vision of those he encounters... These are compelling poems... moving and powerful writing."

Other Poetry

No Laughing Matter

"Roger Elkin's creativity is blooming, and, tended with real craft, it makes for a deeply satisfying read. *No Laughing Matter*... is marked by confident writing on large subjects: a colourful enticing series of poetic vistas.... Elkin's writing is informed, but never over-bearingly so... The beauty of Elkin's writing lies in the authority behind a resonating voice, the wisdom that's scoring the music. We need this kind of poetry, as it helps us to understand more about what it means to live on this small and intricate island."

Will Daunt, *Envoi*

Dog's Eye View